The Alkaline Diet

Delicious pH-Friendly Recipes

Table of Contents

Zucchini Salad with Sundried Tomato Sauce

Almond Cheese and Nori

Green Goodness Smoothie

Red Berry Smoothie

Strawberry Banana Shake

Mango Ginger Apple Salad

Paleo Rise & Shine Smoothie

Green Supreme Smoothie

Cold Carrot Ginger Soup

Avocado Persimmon Salad

Thai Coconut Curry

Pesto Tomato Caprese

Savory Stuffed Peppers

Ginger Orange Burst

Peaches and Spiced Almonds

Sweet Carrot Raisin Salad

Introduction

If you're looking to detox your body, you might want to give the alkaline diet a try. Based on simple scientific principles, the alkaline diet aims to restore acid and base balance in your body. While this sounds pretty complicated, simple guidelines make it much easier to understand and follow. If you're not sure where to start, have a look at the recipes in this book. You don't have to eat your fruit and veggies plain. You can make amazing smoothies, soups and salads. This cookbook contains 30 simple but highly alkalinizing recipes to get you started. Simply follow the guidelines to come up with your own yummy alkalinizing menu. When you see how much extra energy you have by restoring your pH balance, you won't even miss the other foods!

Why the Alkaline Diet?

Our modern lifestyle emphasizes consumption of junk food, meat, dairy and other animal products along with processed foods and grains. These foods, which make up the bulk of many people's diet, have an acidifying effect on the body.

The human body has the amazing ability to auto-regulate vital parameters such as pH (acid/base balance), sodium and sugar levels, water levels, blood pressure and more. Unfortunately, its regulating mechanisms sometimes have long-term detrimental effects on other biological functions.

The human body is naturally slightly alkaline. A pH above 7 indicates alkalinity, while a pH below 7 means the substance is acidic. Our blood needs to stay in the 7.53-7.45 range in order to sustain life. Anything below or above this range can have serious immediate and long-term consequences. The pH scales measures the amount of unbound hydrogen ions in a substance. Some foods break down into more free hydrogen ions than others, while other foods form hydroxyl ions when digested. Hydroxyl ions neutralize acidic (hydrogen) ions and balance the pH.

Problems arise when the pH becomes low enough that the body panics and tries to restore balance by using alkaline minerals from the bones or other structures. On a less dramatic scale, chronic mild acidosis (metabolic acidic state) caused by a lack of hydroxyl-forming foods and an excess of hydrogen ion-forming foods creates an acidic build-up inside the cells, preventing them from accomplishing their duties properly. The results are fatigue, increased chances of illness such as cancer, and nutritional deficiencies.

The alkaline diet helps restore pH balance in cells, blood and other body fluids. There are many variants of this diet, and while they don't always agree on certain items, the basics are essentially the same: meat and animal products such as dairy, eggs, organ meats and broth, vegetable oils, legumes, all grains (except certain forms of sprouted grains and millet), processed sugars and sugar in general form acid compounds when broken down. These acidic compounds build up in cells and blood, causing fatigue and other health problems.

For optimum energy and detox, most versions of the alkaline diet suggest an 80/20 split: 80% alkalinizing foods and 20% other foods. Not all alkalinizing or acidifying foods are on the same level, and some are more beneficial than others. Once you recover from years of acidosis, you can reintroduce acidifying foods in your diet to reach an approximate 60/40 split: 60% alkalinizing foods and 40% acid-forming foods. The goal is to avoid acid build-up and the use of important body minerals to compensate for excessive acid.

Foods are best consumed fresh or raw for maximum benefits. Coconut oil is universally regarded as alkalinizing. Fresh fruit and veggies, almonds, spices, stevia, fermented tofu and apple cider vinegar are considered staples on the alkaline diet. The recipes contained in this book are highly alkalinizing, meaning they contain either exclusively alkaline-forming foods or a tiny amount of acidifying foods. Keep in mind that these do not refer to the food's actual acidity: lemons and limes are considered alkalinizing.

Foods to Avoid

You will usually want to avoid:

- Meat, fish, seafood, poultry and their by-products: meat is one of the most acidifying foods and should be avoided during detox. It can be consumed in very small amounts if properly balanced with alkalinizing veggies.
- Eggs, milk, cheese, butter, ghee, lard: these animal products form acid compounds when digested
- Vegetable oils: safflower, canola, corn, flax, sesame, etc. Coconut oil is universally accepted, and some versions of the alkaline diet also include olive oil in the list of allowed foods.
- Chocolate, cocoa, alcohol, artificial sweeteners, coffee, tea
- Junk food and pre-packaged food
- Sugar in all its forms: maple syrup, pasteurized honey, agave nectar, turbinado sugar, table sugar, etc. The exceptions in some versions of the alkaline diet are blackstrap molasses and raw honey. In any case, consume with moderation.
- Grains: wheat, oats, rice, wild rice, triticale, sorghum, corn, rye, barley, etc. Certain types of sprouted grains are sometimes accepted. Millet is generally regarded as alkaline-forming and can be used.
- Legumes: beans, peas, chickpeas, soy (except fermented tofu), lentils, etc. String beans and green fresh peas are fine.
- Blueberries, cranberries and canned fruit, pickles, olives, winter squash, although not every version agrees on these.

Paleo Coconut Drink

Prep time: 5 minutes

INGREDIENTS

¼ cup coconut milk

1 banana

1 cup strawberries

½ cup ice cubes

INSTRUCTIONS

1. Remove stems from strawberries.
2. Combine all the ingredients in a blender and blend until pureed.
3. Serve.

Raspberry Blend

Prep time: 5 minutes

INGREDIENTS

¼ cup coconut milk

1 banana

½ cup raspberries

½ cup peaches

½ cup ice cubes

INSTRUCTIONS

1. Remove pits from peaches.
2. Combine all the ingredients in a blender and blend until pureed.
3. Serve.

Plantain Fries

Prep Time: 10 minutes

Cook Time: 15

Servings: 1

INGREDIENTS

1 large green plantain

Celtic sea salt, to taste

1/2 lime (optional)

coconut oil (for cooking)

INSTRUCTIONS

1. Bring pot of salted water to boil over medium heat. Heat large pan over medium-high heat. Coat with coconut oil.
2. Cut off ends of plantain. Carefully cut through peel down length of plantain on 4 sides. Remove thick peel.
3. Cut plantain on sharp diagonal to make long angled 1/4 inch slices. Add to boiling water. Cook about 5 minutes, until tender but not mushy.
4. Drain plantains on paper towels and pat to dry. Slice plantains into strips.
5. Add par cooked plantain strips to hot oil. Cook about 2 - 4 minutes on each side, until golden brown and cooked through. Turn with tongs or slotted spoon half way through cooking.
6. Remove cooked plantain from pan and drain on clean paper towels. Transfer to serving dish.

7. Sprinkle with salt, to taste. Cut lime into wedges and squeeze over dish (optional).

8. Serve hot with lime wedges.

Carrot Fries

Prep Time: 5 minutes

Cook Time: 30 minutes

Servings: 2

INGREDIENTS

3 large carrots

2 tablespoons coconut oil

1 rosemary sprig

1/2 teaspoon Celtic sea salt

INSTRUCTIONS

1. Preheat oven to 450 degrees F. Line sheet pan with parchment or coat lightly with coconut oil.
2. Cut carrots in half crosswise, then slice into 1/4 inch strips. Add to medium mixing bowl with oil. Mince rosemary and add to bowl. Toss to coat.
3. Spread carrots on sheet pan in well-spaced single layer. Sprinkle salt over carrots and bake for 10 minutes.
4. Carefully turn carrots over with tongs or spatula. Bake another 10 minutes, or until golden and crispy.
5. Remove sheet pan from oven and transfer carrots to serving dish.
6. Serve hot with your favorite condiment or sauce.

Buttery Cauliflower Popcorn

Prep Time: 5 minutes

Cook Time: 30 minutes

Servings: 4

INGREDIENTS

1 head cauliflower

3 tablespoons coconut oil (melted)

Celtic sea salt, to taste

Pinch cayenne pepper (optional)

Pinch garlic powder (optional)

INSTRUCTIONS

1. Preheat oven to 400 degrees F. Line sheet pan with parchment or baking mat.
2. Remove thick stem from cauliflower, then cut larger florets into golf ball sized pieces.
3. Add cauliflower florets to medium mixing bowl or container with well-fitting lid. Add 1 1/2 tablespoons oil, salt and spices, to taste.
4. Secure lid on container and shake well until cauliflower is evenly coated.
5. Spread seasoned florets in single layer on prepared sheet pan. Bake for 30 - 40 minutes, turning every 10 minutes, until evenly golden brown.
6. Remove from oven transfer to serving dish. Drizzle on remaining oil. Sprinkle with salt and spices, to taste.

7. Serve warm.

Chilled Mango Soup

Prep Time: 10 minutes

Servings: 4

INGREDIENTS

3 large ripe mangoes

1 large onion (yellow, white or sweet)

2 inch piece fresh ginger

2 chili peppers

Cold water

INSTRUCTIONS

1. Peel mangoes, then carefully slice around pit. Peel and grate ginger. Peel and roughly chop onion. Remove stems and seeds from chilis, if desired.
2. Add to food processor or high-speed blender and process until smooth, about 2 minutes. Add enough water to reach desired consistency.
3. Transfer to serving dish and serve chilled.

Mexican Tomato Soup

Prep Time: 10 minutes

Cook Time: 40 minutes

Servings: 4

INGREDIENTS

2 cans (14.5 oz) organic crushed tomatoes

2 cans (11.5) organic tomato juice

5 large tomatoes (or 10 plum tomatoes)

1/2 cup coconut milk

1 red bell pepper (or 1/4 cup roasted red peppers, jarred)

1/4 red onion (or yellow or white onion)

2 garlic cloves

1/2 Serrano chili pepper (or other chili pepper) (optional)

1 tablespoon tapioca flour (or arrowroot powder)

2 tablespoons fresh Mexican oregano (or 1 teaspoon dried oregano)

2 large basil leaves

Celtic sea salt, to taste

1 small bunch cilantro (for garnish)

2 tablespoons coconut oil

INSTRUCTIONS

1. Juice tomatoes and set aside.
2. Roast red bell pepper over stove burner or until broiler, if using. Turn to char on all sides until skins sears. Rub off blackened skin. Cut in half and remove seeds, stem and veins.

3. Heat medium pot over medium-high heat. Add fat to hot pot.

4. Peel onion and garlic. Dice onion, roasted and red pepper. Mince garlic and Serrano pepper (optional). Add to hot oiled pot and sauté until fragrant, about 2 minutes.

5. Add tapioca and coconut milk. Stir to combine. Let cook about 2 minutes.

6. Chiffon (thinly slice) basil. Add to pot with tomato juice, crushed tomatoes, oregano, pepper and salt, to taste. Stir to combine.

7. Bring to simmer, then reduce heat to low. Simmer and reduce about 30 minutes, or until desired consistency is reached.

8. Transfer to serving dish. Chop cilantro and sprinkle over dish for garnish.

9. Serve hot.

Spinach Artichoke Soup

Prep Time: 5 minutes

Cook Time: 30 minutes

Servings: 4

INGREDIENTS

2 cups vegetable broth

1 can (13.5 oz) full-fat coconut milk

4 cups spinach leaves

1 1/2 cups artichoke hearts (canned or jarred, drained)

1/2 small onion (yellow or white)

1 garlic clove

2 teaspoons Celtic sea salt

1 tablespoon coconut oil

INSTRUCTIONS

1. Heat medium pot over medium heat. Add fat to hot pot.
2. Peel and thinly slice onion. Peel and finely grate or mince garlic. Add to hot oiled pot and sauté until tender and translucent, about 5 minutes.
3. Fill pot with spinach and stir to wilt. Continue until all spinach is added. Stir in salt.
4. Chop artichoke hearts and add to pot with veggie broth and coconut milk. Stir to combine.
5. Bring to simmer and heat through, about 8 - 10 minutes.
6. Transfer to serving dish and serve hot.

Cream of Mushroom Soup

Prep Time: 5 minutes

Cook Time: 30 minutes

Servings: 4

INGREDIENTS

3 cups vegetable broth

1 can (13.5 oz) full-fat coconut milk

4 cups mushrooms (white, baby bella, etc.)

1/2 onion (yellow or white)

1 garlic clove

2 teaspoons Celtic sea salt

2 tablespoons coconut oil

INSTRUCTIONS

1. Heat large pot over medium-high heat. Add 1 tablespoon fat to hot pot.

2. Slice 1 cup mushrooms and add to pot. Sauté until lightly browned and tender, about 5 minutes. Remove from pot and set aside.

3. Add remaining fat to hot pot. Reduce heat to medium.

4. Peel and chop onions and garlic. Add to hot oiled pot and sauté until fragrant and lightly browned, about 5 minutes.

5. Add whole mushrooms to pot and sauté until lightly browned and tender, about 8 - 10 minutes.

6. Transfer mushrooms, onion and garlic to food processor or high-speed blender with vegetable broth, coconut milk, salt and pepper. Process until smooth, about 1 - 2 minutes.

7. Or add vegetable broth, coconut milk and salt to pot and purée with immersion blender.

8. Heat pot over medium heat. Add reserved sliced mushrooms to pot and stir to combine.

9. Bring to simmer and heat through, about 8 - 10 minutes.

10. Transfer to serving dish and serve hot.

Baked Sweet Plantains

Prep Time: 5 minutes

Cook Time: 20 minutes

Servings: 1

INGREDIENTS

1 ripe yellow plantain

1 tablespoon stevia

2 tablespoons water

1 teaspoon coconut oil

1/2 teaspoon ground cinnamon

INSTRUCTIONS

1. Preheat oven to 400 degrees F. Line baking pan with parchment, or lightly coat with coconut oil.
2. Cut plantain into 3/4 inch slices. Remove peel from each slice.
3. Toss plantains in small bowl with stevia, water, oil and cinnamon.
4. Arrange plantains in single layer on baking pan. Bake 10 minutes, then turn over and bake another 10 minutes, or until plantains are golden brown and tender.
5. Serve warm.

Ants On A Log

Prep Time: 5 minutes

Cook Time: 5 minutes

Servings: 2

INGREDIENTS

3 celery stalks

2 tablespoons raisins

Almond Butter

1 cup almonds

1 teaspoon coconut oil

1/2 teaspoon ground cinnamon

INSTRUCTIONS

1. Add almonds, cinnamon, and coconut oil to food processor or bullet blender. Process until smooth. Let mixture rest between periods of processing to reach desired consistency, if necessary.

2. Cut celery stakes into thirds and fill wells with *Almond Butter*. Place raisins on almond butter.

3. Serve room temperature. Or refrigerate 10 minutes and serve chilled.

Grilled Pineapple Fruit Salad

Prep Time: 5 minutes

Cook Time: 10 minutes

Servings: 4

INGREDIENTS

1/2 pineapple

1 peach

1 cup fresh cherries

1 orange

1 tablespoon fresh mint leaves

Half lemon

INSTRUCTIONS

1. Heat griddle or grill over medium-high heat. Lightly coat with coconut oil.
2. Peel and core pineapple. Cut into half inch slices. Place slice on griddle and grill about 4 - 5 minutes on each side, until grill marks appear and sugars caramelized.
3. Cut peach in half and grill flesh side down for about 5 minutes.
4. Pit cherries and slice in half. Peel orange and cut flesh from white cellulose film and pith.
5. Chop pineapple and peach. Add to medium mixing bowl with cherries and orange wedges. Chiffon mint. Add to bowl and squeeze on lemon juice. Toss to combine.
6. Serve room temperature. Or refrigerate and serve chilled.

Piña Colada Smoothie

Prep Time: 5 minutes

Cook Time: 5 minutes

Servings: 2

INSTRUCTIONS

1 large banana

1 cup pineapple chunks (fresh, frozen or canned)

2 tablespoons flaked coconut

1 cup coconut milk

1 cup ice (crushed preferably)

DIRECTIONS

1. Add banana, pineapple, coconut, coconut milk and ice to highs-speed blender. Process until smooth.

2. Pour into chilled glasses and serve immediately.

Simple Guacamole

Prep Time: 5 minutes

Cook Time: 5 minutes

Servings: 4

INGREDIENTS

2 avocados

1 shallot

1 small tomato

1 bunch cilantro

Half lime

2 teaspoons paprika

1/2 teaspoon ground cumin

1/2 teaspoon sea salt

INSTRUCTIONS

1. Peel and finely dice shallot. Dice tomato and cilantro. Add to small mixing bowl.

2. Slice avocados in half, pit, and scoop flesh into bowl. Add 1 teaspoon paprika, 1/2 teaspoon cumin and 1/2 teaspoon salt.

3. Mash avocado and mix ingredients well with fork. Transfer to serving dish and squeeze on juice of half a lime. Sprinkle with remaining teaspoon of paprika.

4. Serve immediately. Or refrigerate 30 minutes, and serve chilled.

Zucchini Salad with Sundried Tomato Sauce

Prep Time: 20 minutes*

Servings: 2

INGREDIENTS

1 medium zucchini

1 tomato

5 sundried tomatoes

1 garlic clove

2 fresh basil leaves

1 tablespoon raw virgin coconut oil (or 2 tablespoons warm water)

1/4 teaspoon sea salt

INSTRUCTIONS

1. Run zucchini through spiralizer, slice into long, thin shreds with knife, or use vegetable peeler to make flat, thin slices. Sprinkle with a pinch of salt and gently toss to coat.

2. Add tomato, sundried tomatoes, peeled garlic, basil, coconut oil or warm water, and remaining salt and pepper to food processor or bullet blender. Process until sauce of desired consistency forms.

3. Transfer zucchini pasta to serving bowls. Top with tomato sauce and serve immediately.

4. Or refrigerate for 20 minutes and serve chilled.

Almond Cheese and Nori

Prep Time: 15 minutes*

Servings: 2

INGREDIENTS

1 cup raw almonds*

1/4 cup water

2 tablespoons coconut oil

1 tablespoon lemon juice

1 tablespoon raw apple cider vinegar

1 garlic clove

1/4 teaspoon paprika

1/4 teaspoon ground black pepper

1/2 teaspoon sea salt

4 - 6 sheets dried nori (seaweed paper)

INSTRUCTIONS

1. *For *Almond Cheese*, soak almonds in enough water to cover overnight. Drain and rinse. Pop off skins and discard.

2. Add soaked almonds, water, coconut oil, lemon juice, vinegar, peeled garlic, salt and spices to food processor or bullet blender and process until smooth. Add a few extra tablespoons of water if necessary to achieve thick but smooth consistency. Transfer *Almond Cheese* to serving dish.

3. Cut nori into small sheets and serve with *Almond Cheese*.

Green Goodness Smoothie

Prep Time: 5 minutes

Servings: 2

INGREDIENTS

2 cups spinach

2 whole kale leaves (1 cup chopped)

1 banana

1 green apple

1/2 cup green grapes

1 cup water (or fresh almond milk)

INSTRUCTIONS

1. Remove stems and ribs from kale. Core apple and dice. Peel banana.
2. Add water (or almond milk), banana and grapes to full sized blender. Process until solids are broken down.
3. Add greens and pulse on low for 30 seconds to break down. Then process on high for 1 minute, until smooth.
4. Pour into serving glasses and serve immediately.
5. Or chill in refrigerator for 20 minutes, blend for a few seconds to incorporate separated liquid, then pour into serving glasses and serve chilled.

Red Berry Smoothie

Prep Time: 5 minutes

Servings: 1

INGREDIENTS

1 cup strawberries

1/2 cup red raspberries

1/4 cup pitted cherries

1/4 cup cherry tomatoes

1/2 - 1 cup water (or fresh nut milk)

Juice of 1 beet (optional)

INSTRUCTIONS

1. Remove leaves from strawberries and chop. Add to full sized blender with raspberries, cherries, tomatoes and beet juice (optional).
2. Add 1/2 cup water and pulse on low for 30 seconds to break down. Add more water if necessary. Then process on high for 30 seconds to 1 minute, until smooth.
3. Pour into serving glasses and serve immediately.
4. Or chill in refrigerator for 20 minutes, blend for a few seconds to incorporate separated liquid, then pour into serving glasses and serve chilled.

Strawberry Banana Shake

Prep Time: 5 minutes*

Cook Time: 0 minutes

Servings: 1

INGREDIENTS

1 banana

1 cup strawberries

1/2 - 1 cup water

Meat of 1/2 fresh coconut (or 1/2 cup unsweetened flaked or shredded coconut)

INSTRUCTIONS

1. *Soak flaked coconut in water for at least 4 hours.
2. Add fresh or soaked flaked coconut and water to high-speed blender. Process on high until smooth, about 1 minute.
3. Strain coconut mixture through nut milk bag or a few layers of cheese cloth. Squeeze out all excess liquid. Reserve coconut milk. Dry excess coconut, process until finely ground, and use as coconut flour.
4. Remove leaves from strawberries and chop. Peel banana.
5. Add coconut milk to blender with fruit and process on high until smooth.
6. Pour into serving glass and serve immediately.

7. Or chill in refrigerator for 20 minutes, blend for a few seconds to incorporate separated liquid, then pour into serving glass and serve chilled.

Mango Ginger Apple Salad

Prep Time: 5 minutes

Servings: 2

INSTRUCTIONS

1 ripe mango

1 granny smith apple

1/4 cup raw almonds

1 inch piece fresh ginger

1/2 teaspoon ground ginger

INGREDIENTS

1. Slice mango in half around pit. Peel flesh and dice. Add to small mixing bowl.
2. Core apple and dice. Peel ginger and mince. Add to bowl with ground ginger.
3. Roughly chop almonds and add to bowl.
4. Mix well and serve immediately. Or refrigerate 20 minutes and serve chilled.

Paleo Rise & Shine Smoothie

Prep time: 5 minutes

INGREDIENTS

1 handful spinach

½ avocado

1 banana

1 large stalk celery

1 tbsp coconut oil

1 tsp cinnamon

1 cup water

INSTRUCTIONS

1. Slice avocado in half and remove the nut. Break the banana into small pieces and chop the celery into small pieces.
2. Combine all ingredients except for the spinach into a blender. Blend them until pureed, then add spinach and blend until pureed.
3. Serve or chill and then serve.

Green Supreme Smoothie

Prep Time: 5 minutes*

Servings: 1

INGREDIENTS

1 cup chopped kale

1/2 cup watercress

1 banana (frozen chunks)

1 green apple

1/2 avocado

1 1/2 cups almond milk

2 - 4 tablespoons stevia

INSTRUCTIONS

1. *Peel banana, then chop and freeze.
2. Remove any stems and ribs from kale. Peel apple if preferred, then core and dice.
3. Slice avocado in half and scoop flesh of pitted half into high-speed blender. Add remaining ingredients and process until smooth, about 1 - 2 minutes.
4. Pour into large glass and serve immediately.

Cold Carrot Ginger Soup

Prep Time: 10 minutes

Servings: 2

INGREDIENTS

3 large carrots

1/2 cup fresh young coconut meat (about 1/2 young coconut)

1/4 cup raw pine nuts (or raw almonds)

1/2 - 1 inch piece fresh ginger

2 sprigs fresh cilantro

1 tablespoon raw apple cider vinegar

Water (or coconut milk)

INSTRUCTIONS

1. Remove cilantro leaves from stems and add to highs-speed blender. Juice ginger, or peel and finely grate. Add to blender with pine nuts, coconut, and apple cider vinegar.

2. Juice carrots, or add to food processor or high-speed blender and process until smooth, about 2 minutes. Add enough water or coconut milk to reach desired consistency.

3. Pour into serving bowls and serve immediately.

Avocado Persimmon Salad

Prep Time: 10 minutes*

Servings: 2

INGREDIENTS

2 persimmons

1 avocado

1 medium cucumber

1/2 sweet onion

2 tablespoons raw coconut oil

2 tablespoon lemon juice (or lime juice or raw apple cider vinegar)

1/4 teaspoon Celtic sea salt

INSTRUCTIONS

1. Peel and seed cucumber if preferred, then dice. Peel persimmons if preferred, then chop. Peel sweet onions and cut in half. Thinly slice. Add to medium mixing bowl.
2. Cut avocado in half and remove pit. Dice peel in flesh and scoop into bowl.
3. Add oil, lemon juice and salt. Toss to coat evenly
4. Transfer to serving dishes and serve immediately.
5. *Or refrigerate for 20 minutes and serve chilled.

Thai Coconut Curry

Prep Time: 20 minutes

Servings: 2

INGREDIENTS

1 tomato

1 carrot

1/2 red pepper

1/2 lemon

1/2 mango

2 cups cauliflower florets

1/2 small onion

1 teaspoon Celtic sea salt

Coconut Curry Sauce

1/2 cup fresh coconut

1/2 lemon

1 lemongrass stem

1 inch piece fresh ginger

1 garlic clove

1 tablespoon fresh curry leaves

Medium bunch fresh parsley

1/2 teaspoon red pepper flakes

1 teaspoon Celtic sea salt

Water

INSTRUCTIONS

1. Seed and chop bell pepper. Seed tomato if preferred, then chop. Dice carrot. Add to medium mixing bowl. Add juice of 1/2 lemon and 1/2 teaspoon salt. Mix and set aside.

2. For *Coconut Curry Sauce*, peel ginger and garlic. Remove coconut flesh from shell and chop. Remove half of parsley from stem. Add to food processor or high-speed blender with lemongrass, lemon juice, curry leaves, salt and red pepper. Process until smooth and creamy, about 1 - 2 minutes. Add enough water to reach desired consistency.

3. Add *Coconut Curry Sauce* to mixing bowl with veggies. Toss to coat and refrigerate at least 10 minutes.

4. Peel onion. Add cauliflower and onion to food processor with shredding attachment and process to "rice." Or mince cauliflower and onion. Add to medium mixing bowl with 1/2 teaspoon salt and mix to combine.

5. Cut mango in half around pit, peel and dice. Chop remaining parsley.

6. Plate "rice" mixture and top with *Coconut Curry Sauce* . Sprinkle mango and parsley over curry. Serve immediately.

Pesto Tomato Caprese

Prep Time: 5 minutes

Servings: 2

INGREDIENTS

1 large yellow tomato

1 large red tomato

Small bunch fresh basil

Celtic sea salt, to taste

Crack or ground black pepper, to taste

Basil Pesto

2 cups basil leaves (packed)

1/4 cup raw pine nuts

1/2 - 1/3 cup raw coconut oil

2 garlic cloves

1/2 lemon (or 1 tablespoon raw apple cider vinegar)

1/4 teaspoon Celtic sea salt

INSTRUCTIONS

1. For *Basil Pesto*, peel garlic and add to food processor or high-speed blender with squeeze of 1/2 lemon. Process until finely chopped. Add pine nuts, basil, oil and salt and process until finely ground, about 1 minute.

2. Slice tomatoes and plate in alternating colors. Sprinkle with salt and pepper. Chiffon basil leaves.

3. Spread *Basil Pesto* over tomato slices and top with fresh basil. Serve immediately.

Savory Stuffed Peppers

Prep Time: 15 minutes

Servings: 1

INGREDIENTS

1 medium-large red bell pepper

1/2 cup cauliflower florets

1/4 small white onion (or sweet onion)

1 celery stalk

1 small carrot

Juice of 1/2 lemon

2 sundried tomatoes

2 tablespoons raw tahini (or 3 tablespoon sesame seeds)

1 tablespoon raw oil (coconut, walnut, almond, sesame, etc.)

1 tablespoon raw pumpkin seeds

1 tablespoon raw sunflower seeds

1 tablespoon dried cranberries (or raisins)

1/2 teaspoon ground cumin

1/4 teaspoon ground ginger

1/4 teaspoon paprika

1/2 teaspoon Celtic sea salt

INSTRUCTIONS

1. Add lemon juice and dried cranberries to medium mixing bowl. Set aside.
2. Slice bell pepper in half and remove seeds and veins. Set aside.

3. Add sundried tomatoes, oil, and tahini or sesame seeds to food processor or high-speed blender. Process until smooth and creamy, about 1 - 2 minutes. Add to cranberries.

4. Add cauliflower and onion to food processor with shredding attachment and process to "rice." Or mince cauliflower and onion. Add to mixing bowl.

5. Finely dice carrot and celery and add to bowl. Add pumpkin seeds, sunflower seeds, salt and spices. Mix to combine.

6. Plate bell pepper halves and stuff with "rice" mixture. Serve immediately.

Ginger Orange Burst

Prep Time: 5 minutes

Servings: 1

INGREDIENTS

3 oranges

1/2 grapefruit

3 large carrots

1 inch piece fresh ginger

Water (optional)

INSTRUCTIONS

1. Peel orange , grapefruit and ginger. Separate citrus segments and add to high-speed blender with carrots and ginger. Process until smooth, about 2 minutes. Add enough water to reach desired consistency.
2. Or peel and cut orange and grapefruit in half, and run through juicer with carrots and ginger.
3. Or cut orange and grapefruit in half and juice with citrus juicer. Then run carrots and ginger through juicer and add to citrus juice.
4. Pour into serving glass and serve immediately.

Peaches and Spiced Almonds

Prep Time: 5 minutes

Servings: 1

INGREDIENTS

2 ripe peaches (or nectarines)

4 dried pitted dates

1/3 cup raw almonds

1/4 teaspoon ground cinnamon

1/4 teaspoon ground ginger

1/8 teaspoon vanilla

1/8 teaspoon ground white pepper (or ground black pepper)

INSTRUCTIONS

1. Add dates, almonds vanilla and spices to food processor or high-speed blender. Pulse to coarsely grind, about 1 minute.
2. Cut peaches in half and remove pits. Dice peaches and transfer to serving dish.
3. Sprinkle on almond mixture and serve immediately.

Sweet Carrot Raisin Salad

Prep Time: 5 minutes

Servings: 2

INSTRUCTIONS

2 large carrots

2 tablespoons red raisins

2 tablespoons golden raisins

1/4 cup raw slivered almonds (or sliced almonds)

1/2 small orange (or tangerine)

1/4 teaspoon ground cinnamon

DIRECTIONS

1. Add carrots to food processor with shredding attachment and process, or grate with grater. Add to medium mixing bowl with raisins, almonds and cinnamon.
2. Zest *then* juice orange. Add to carrot mixture and toss to combine.
3. Transfer to serving dishes and serve immediately. Or refrigerate 20 minutes and serve chilled.

Made in the USA
Lexington, KY
19 November 2015